Michael J. Fox

Michael J. Fox

Keith Elliot Greenberg

Lerner Publications Company
Minneapolis

Acknowledgements
This book contains information from a personal interview
with Michael J. Fox conducted by the author, as well as articles
in *Teen Beat, People, Bop,* the *San Juan Star, Us, 16,*
Tiger Beat Star and the *Milwaukee Journal.*

LIBRARY OF CONGRESS CATALOGING-IN-PUBLICATION DATA

Greenberg, Keith Elliot.
  Michael J. Fox.

  Summary: Follows the life and career of the diminutive
Canadian actor who has achieved phenomenal success in both
television and film work.
  1. Fox, Michael J., 1961-   —Juvenile literature. 2. Actors—
Canada—Biography—Juvenile literature. 3. Actors—United States—
Biography—Juvenile literature. [1. Fox, Michael J., 1961-   . 2. Actors
and actresses]
I. Title.
PN2308.F69G74   1986   791.43'028'0924 [B] [92]   86-10518
ISBN 0-8225-1611-X (lib. bdg.)

  2 3 4 5 6 7 8 9 10 96 95 94 93 92 91 90 89 88 87

Contents

Just A Regular Guy

Mick Jagger, lead singer of the Rolling Stones, has his strut. Michael Jackson, creator of such hits as "Beat It" and "Thriller," has his spangly glove. Don Johnson, hero of the "Miami Vice" television show, has his white dinner jacket and black sunglasses.

But Michael J. Fox, the young man responsible for the success of the films *Teen Wolf* and *Back to the Future* and the TV program "Family Ties," has none of the above.

No one can deny that Fox is a superstar. Yet the 5-foot, 4-inch, 120-pound, blue-eyed actor looks like he'd be more comfortable cruising a high school hallway than performing on a Hollywood sound stage. Without any gimmicks, he has risen to the top of the entertainment industry.

Off the set, he remains what he seems—a modest young man who is happily bewildered by all the attention he receives. His sincerity—along with his good looks and acting ability—make him a director's dream. According to filmmaker John Hughes, Fox is "my favorite actor who I've ever worked with....He's a very free guy—he just wings it. That excitement translates on screen."

No actor has made as winning a leap from television to movies since heart-throb John Travolta of "Welcome Back Kotter" sizzled onto the silver screen in the 1978 film *Saturday Night Fever*. Fox has been interviewed by Barbara Walters and Johnny Carson, who are known for seeking out only the cream of the crop. World leaders have praised Michael's work and have met with him. If he wanted to, he could easily put less effort into acting and just rest on his reputation. But that isn't his style. "Family Ties" co-star Justine Bateman observes that Fox aims "to do good work—not just make a big splash."

Having seen hard times while climbing the ladder to fame, Michael realizes that he is lucky to be making a living in one of the world's most competitive professions. "Acting helps me get away from the pressures of just being me," he says. "I can be another character for a while and that's a lot of fun. But mostly, I love acting because it's a great way for me to express my emotions. I tend to be quite an emotional person at times."

He views his fans as being similar to him, describing them as "kids who are open and affectionate. My attitude is that this one paid my rent, that one bought my car,

Michael as Scott Howard in *Teen Wolf.*

that one paid for the hockey tickets." And he appreciates every one.

An Army Brat with Dreams

Although he has an "all-American boy" image, Michael was actually born in Canada, on June 9, 1961. His middle initial is really "A," not "J." The switch was made when Michael began acting. He didn't want people to think he was conceitedly implying "Michael's A Fox."

His father was a Canadian army officer who moved the family all over the provinces before settling in the Vancouver suburb of Burnaby when Michael was eleven. Because the names and faces of the neighbors changed so often, the Foxes—parents Bill and Phyllis, sisters Jackie, Karen and Kelli, and brother Steven—grew extremely close. Michael developed his likable personality making new friends every time he changed his address.

Always one of the shortest children in his class,

Michael sometimes felt insecure about his height. "I guess some of my shyness has carried over from when I was a kid," he says. "I was always short, and then in my teens I gained a lot of weight. I was about five inches shorter and twenty pounds heavier than I am now. You can imagine how I didn't feel too good about myself back then, and some of those self-conscious feelings are still with me. I have a lot more going for me now, though, and I try to keep that in mind."

One of Michael's idols was another little guy, the late Jimmy Cagney, the wise-cracking star of 1930s movies like *Yankee Doodle Dandy* and *The Roaring Twenties*. Like Fox, Cagney made up for his lack of height by turning on the confidence and talent when it was necessary.

Being Canadian, Michael loved playing hockey. He also wrote short stories and took guitar lessons. "I always wanted to do something in the arts," he says. "I was determined to be a musician or a writer or an artist or an actor."

Never did he imagine himself as a comic performer. "I avoided comedy," he recalls. "I was afraid of not being funny. My brother was always the funny one at the dinner table." Fox tries to insert a great deal of Steven's personality into the Alex character on "Family Ties."

When Michael was fifteen, one of his junior high school teachers told him there was an opening for the role of an exceptionally bright ten-year-old on the Canadian Broadcasting Company show "Leo and Me." "I looked amazingly young for my age," he remembers, "and I surprised myself by passing the audition."

"It didn't seem like a big deal. I never had any idea like 'This is it! I'm a star!' I just thought it was interesting to be on TV."

"Leo and Me" lasted two years. Afterward, Fox did radio and stage work. While acting in the play *Shadow Box*, he decided to make entertaining his lifetime career: "Something just clicked in my head. I thought something like 'This is great! I love it! I don't want to do anything else!'"

After *Shadow Box*, Michael portrayed the grandson of Art Carney and Maureen Stapleton in *Letters from Frank*, a television movie filmed in Vancouver. So impressed were the veteran actors with the boy's talent that they nagged him about moving to Los Angeles, where acting jobs were more plentiful.

Michael thought it over. He was scared by the thought of being all alone in a strange city. And he knew he would miss his family. But the words of such respected performers as Carney and Stapleton were weighty. In June, 1979, a few days after his eighteenth birthday, Michael relocated to the City of the Stars.

Family Ties

The first few months in Los Angeles were nerve-wracking. Michael spent endless hours by the telephone, waiting for casting directors to call. Each day, he would go to auditions. "I'd get up every morning and head out for another day of rejection," he says. So many roles seemed to pass him by.

Slowly, work began to come. The parts weren't big ones, but they were a start. Michael played a spoiled gymnast on an episode of "The Love Boat," and made appearances on other television programs like "Teachers

Michael J. Fox and Justine Bateman

Only," "Lewis and Clark," "Trapper John, M.D.," "Lou Grant," and "Family." He acted in the films *Midnight Madness* and *Class of 1984*. Beating out three hundred other candidates, he won a role on the TV series "Palmerstown, U.S.A."

Before the fall 1982 television season began filming, Fox was shown the script for a new program called "Family Ties." The plot pitted a basically conservative teenager against his ultra-liberal parents. Because it was a comedy, Michael was hesitant to join the show. "Again, I was afraid that I wouldn't be funny," he says. "I also figured that most situation comedies were silly. But the script blew me away. It was gentle with its lack of insult humor. I liked the conflict of two different schools of thought. It was nice how, in the end, you learned how people could see through their differences. It made me think that we're really ripping ourselves off if we don't try to understand and respect other people's feelings."

He passed the audition for the role of Alex, the opinionated teenager, and soon was charming a large percentage of America through the TV screen. Although critics rave that Fox "made" the series, he commends his co-stars: "Big sister" Justine Bateman is "so full of energy and budding talent. A lot of people can act, but she is a real actress." "Little sister" Tina Youthers can "knock you out of a scene. You say, 'For a little kid, this girl is a real professional.'" "Mother" Meredith Baxter Birney brings "a sense of family to the show. When her television character is concerned with Alex, I can see Meredith being concerned with her son, Ted."

"Father" Michael Gross can "turn a dull scene into something great" with one bit of advice.

Fox stresses that there is little similarity between him and Alex. "I think that Alex wouldn't approve of actors. He's such a businessman. He'd probably think acting was a silly way to make money.

"Personally, I never related much to numbers. When I'm holding the *Wall Street Journal* on the set, I have to be careful I'm not holding it upside down.

"Another difference is that I'm Canadian. And, being Canadian, I have very few opinions about American politics."

He does admit that Alex has influenced his fashion sense. "I used to dress in jeans and t-shirts all the time, but now I can appreciate a nice Brooks Brothers brand tie. I might not know how to *tie* it, but I can appreciate it."

The spring after the show began, Michael made his first visit to New York City, where a sobbing admirer shrieked, "Marry me!" The actor was bewildered. "I'd be lying if I didn't admit that it felt nice," he says. "But you have to take these things the right way. I mean, every actor likes to have visible evidence that his work is affecting people—but this was truly ridiculous."

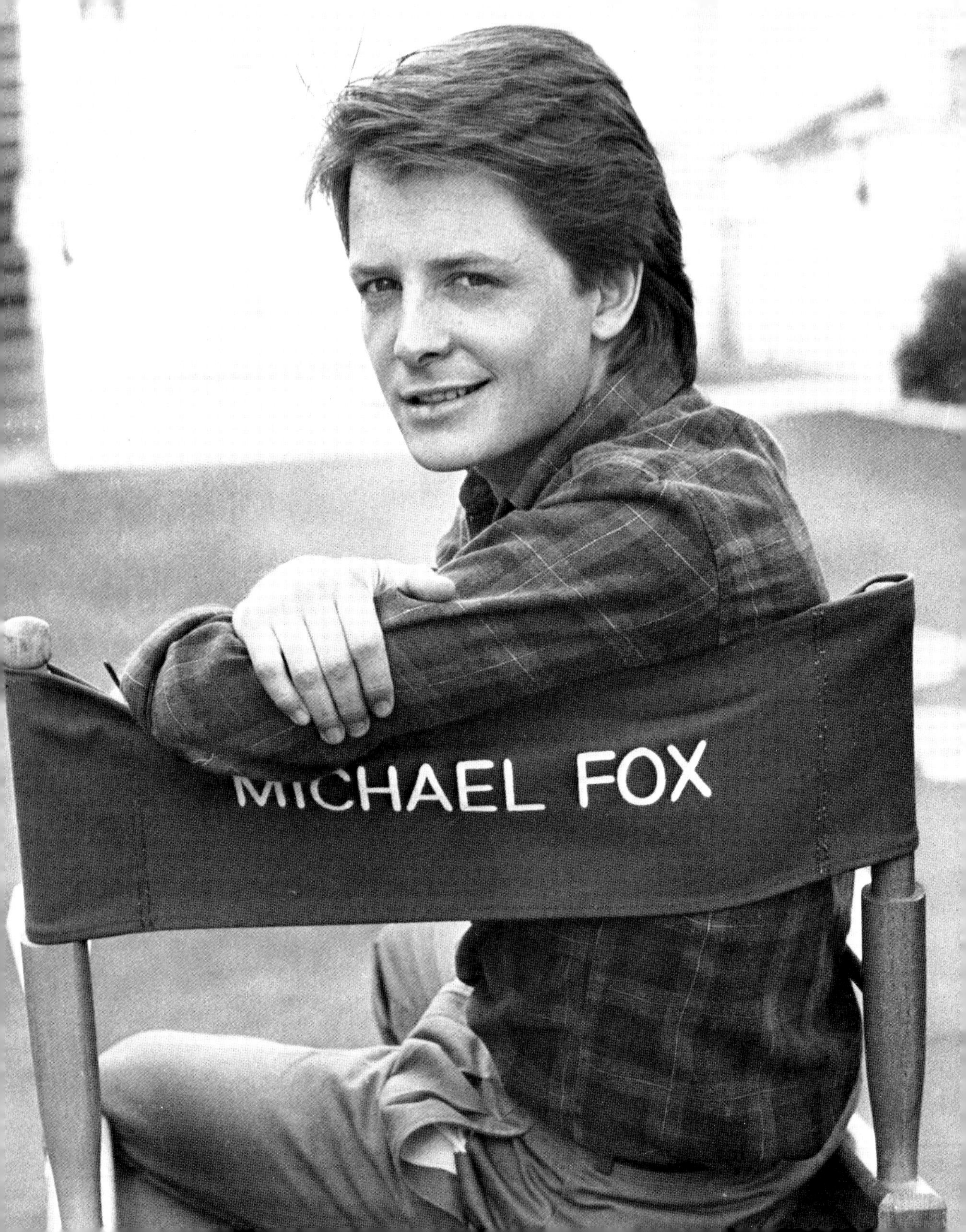
MICHAEL FOX

King of Comedy

Michael J. Fox became a superstar in the summer of 1985, following the success of his movies *Teen Wolf* and *Back to the Future*.

Originally, he was not taken with the title of the movie *Teen Wolf*, the story of a young man who turns into a werewolf. However, as was the case with "Family Ties," he grew fond of the script. Although the teenage werewolf in the film certainly *looks* vicious, he cares more about romance and sports than about harming others. Fox liked this gentle twist on an old horror movie concept.

Reviewers were kind to cast members James Hampton, Susan Ursitti and Jerry Levine, but their greatest praise went to Michael. Said Ira Hellman in *People* magazine:

"Fox's performance is remarkably controlled. He has a natural comic ability that adds a little flair to every situation."

Back to the Future, the tale of a boy who travels back in time to the 1950s and helps his parents fall in love, was initially supposed to star Eric Stoltz. When producers decided that he "didn't have the vulnerability or youthfulness for the part," Michael was chosen for the lead role.

While the movie was being made, Michael worked round-the-clock, laboring on the set of "Family Ties" during the day and on *Back to the Future* at night. He jokes that the frantic pace had a brain-scrambling effect: "You know how your dreams are peopled with family and friends? Well, imagine all those people in your dreams, plus two full crews, two directors, like six producers, then the public. My dreams looked like the Olympics."

Back to the Future was the summer's biggest box office hit, grossing $180 million. *Teen Wolf* took in $33 million. As a result, more and more viewers tuned to "Family Ties" just to see Fox. The series was the second most-watched program of the fall 1985 season, after "The Cosby Show."

In 1986, Michael was nominated for an Emmy for television achievement. "Family Ties" and *Back to the Future* were nominees for People's Choice Awards, for which 193 million average citizens vote.

Among other honors Fox has received:

Most Exciting New Star of 1985—presented by the National Association of Theater Owners.

Movie Star of the Year (1985)—by the readers of *16* magazine.

Male Discovery of the Year (1985)—by the Hollywood Women's Press Corps.

One of America's ten Best Dressed Men—by the National Hairdressers and Cosmetologists Association.

Michael was overjoyed to introduce the world to his parents when he was interviewed by Barbara Walters for the ABC television network. He told Walters about his admiration for his brother Steven as well.

During her visit to the United States, England's Princess Diana met Michael when both were guests of President Ronald Reagan at the White House.

But perhaps Fox's biggest thrill occurred October 24, 1985. As part of a fund-raising effort for the restoration of the Statue of Liberty, his idol Jimmy Cagney had been asked to tell his version of the Irish-American experience. The elderly star wrote his feelings down—then requested that Michael read them for him on television. On October 24, the young actor was honored to oblige.

Taking It Easy

Michael doesn't have much free time. Between making movies and working on "Family Ties," he has about four days off per year. He realizes the importance of conserving his energy, and is hardly what one would call a "party animal." However, his boyhood friends in Burnaby refuse to believe this, and they drag him to nightclubs whenever he visits his home town. When the binge is over, Fox says, "I'm so wiped out that I fall back on my mother's couch and sleep for three days."

Even with his hectic schedule, he manages to find

Michael J. Fox and Nancy McKeon

23

the time to help various charities. He is national chairman of a group dedicated to increasing public awareness about spina bifida, a crippling birth defect.

His home in the Laurel Canyon section of Los Angeles includes three bedrooms, fireplaces, hardwood floors, a black-bottomed pool and a spa. Although he is a millionaire and could afford almost any piece of furniture, his favorite seat is a worn, corn-colored couch, which he finds ideal for watching football on television.

When he is alone, he reads horror stories, draws, and goes through his fan mail. It would be impossible to answer each of the 21,000 fan letters he receives every week, but he wants it known that every letter is appreciated. "I never get tired of getting letters from people who like my work," he told a journalist. "And you can print that!"

Like the characters in his movies, Michael loves rock 'n' roll, particularly the music of ZZ Top. Their song, "La Grange," can frequently be heard blasting from his stereo speakers.

Michael follows the example of physical fitness set by "Family Ties" co-star Meredith Baxter Birney, who has run in the New York Marathon. He swims, skis, plays basketball, and lifts weights under the supervision of a personal trainer.

Recently, Fox purchased a black Jeep and black Datsun 300 ZX. If his favorite hockey team, the Vancouver Canucks, is in Los Angeles for a game against the Kings, it is a safe bet that Fox will drive over to the L.A. Forum to watch the action.

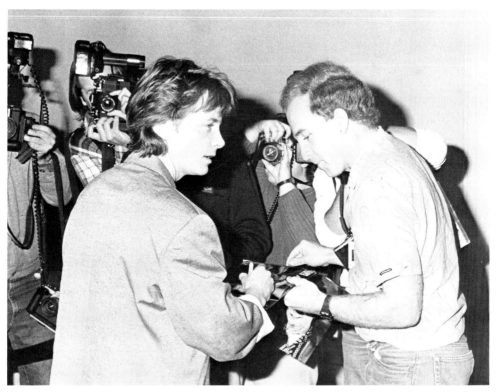

Fans and reporters greet Michael with cameras and autograph requests wherever he goes.

As one would guess, many people try to get close to the actor. But he knows who his friends *really* are: "I learned to make the distinction in my mind between business associates, good acquaintances, and true friends. I don't have to choose—I can feel it when a friendship is right."

He is still close to many he grew up with. "Most of the guys from home now work in the railroad or in construction," he says, "but I get along with them fine,

Michael with Tracy Pollan, who portrays Ellen Reed, his girlfriend on "Family Ties."

because really I'm just doing a job." Fox naturally has many friends in show biz. "We speak the same language," he says.

His social calendar is not jammed with as many dates as fans think: "I know it may be hard to believe, but

I'm quite shy around girls. Even if I like a girl a lot, it usually takes me months to ask her out. I guess you could say I'm slightly bashful." Besides, he claims, he'd rather spend his time "making people laugh than chasing girls all over the place."

Michael's ideal date is a frank woman with a sense of humor. "I like a girl who is honest and funny. There's so much in the world to be depressed about, I think it takes a lot of strength to make others happy. And when you're laughing, you're at your best."

While gossip columnists have linked Fox romantically with Nancy McKeon, star of the television series "The Facts of Life," he calls her his "best friend." They met in 1985, while making a television production called *Poison Ivy* in which they played summer camp counselors, and they constantly communicate. Says Nancy: "I enjoy Michael's company a lot. He makes me laugh and feel comfortable. Although we don't see each other much, we keep in contact somehow, either with phone calls or sending little messages to each other."

Michael has also been seen out on the town with Helen Slater, star of *Supergirl*. He keeps the gossip columnists busy and the fans wondering.

Fox's Future

   Michael's success in motion pictures has caused many to speculate that he will leave "Family Ties" shortly. Fox has other ideas. "I love being Alex. I'll stay on with 'Family Ties' as long as there is a 'Family Ties.'"

   In March 1986, work began on *Light of Day*, a film that features Michael in his first major dramatic role. It tells of the life of Joe Rasnick, a twenty-two-year-old factory worker who plays in a weekend bar band with his sister. Michael claims the character is more like

"Marty McFly" of *Back to the Future*

Michael celebrated the completion of *Light of Day* **with co-star Joan Jett, who could bring real experience as a rock star to her role in Michael's band.**

him than any other he's played. He says, "If I wasn't making a living as an actor, I'd be playing bad guitar in some bad bars around Vancouver."

Joe Rasnick is tougher than the innocent characters Fox has portrayed in the past. Michael hopes fans will see that there are many sides to his personality—that he can play other roles besides open-faced, high school boys. Paul Schrader, director of the film, already knows this. Michael's "a likable actor," Schrader says, "but he doesn't have to be so clean-scrubbed."

The original title of the film was *Born In The U.S.A.*

Like the album of that name by Bruce Springsteen, the movie paints a picture of working-class America. Springsteen agreed to write the film's theme song, which shares the same title as the production.

How important is Fox's involvement to the project? Producer Rob Cohen says that casting Fox as the lead gave the film life. "The minute we had him," Cohen says, "we had just about every studio in town calling and trying to get" the movie.

After he completed his dramatic film, he began working on a romantic comedy called *Private Affairs*. He plays an awkward but ambitious twenty-two-year-old who moves to New York City from Kansas to tackle the world of big business.

Other projects include a *Back to the Future* sequel, scheduled for release in 1988; a comedy about the first male students to attend Vassar College; *The Kirk Crocker Story*, a non-fiction television movie about a young man radiation-poisoned by his father; and a TV movie that has special meaning to the entertainer: *Young Jimmy Cagney*. About playing his hero, Michael says, "It's the role of a lifetime." Producer Robert Halmi observed, "Jimmy and Michael have a mutual admiration society."

Michael J. Fox is a kid who seems to have it all. But there are still fantasies he hasn't realized. Some involve dramatics: he'd like to appear in a Broadway show and write a screenplay. One involves sports: he wants to meet the Vancouver Canucks. His eyes sparkle when he states, "If I could skate around with them on the ice during a practice, it would be like a dream come true."

Michael with his "parents" of "Family Ties," Meredith Baxter Birney and Michael Gross.

Photo credits:

AP/Wide World Photos, pp. 1, 18, 30
Frank Edwards/Fotos International, pp. 2, 25, 32
Darlene Hammond/Pictorial Parade, p. 6
Collectors Book Store, pp. 9, 28
Phil Roach/Photoreporters, p. 10
Retna Ltd., p. 14
Walter McBride/Retna Ltd., p. 22
Fotos International, p. 26

Front cover photo by Geoffrey Croft/Retna Ltd.
Back cover photo by Fotos International

S